PEOPLE and the PLANET

Torrey Maloof

Consultant

Catherine Hollinger, CID, CLIA
EPA WaterSense Partner
Environmental Consultant

Image Credits: p.27 (bottom) Ambient Images Inc./Alamy; p.5 (top) Frances Roberts/Alamy; pp.14–15 (background) James Osmond/Alamy; p.11 (bottom left) Premium Stock Photography GmbH/Alamy; p.11 (top) Stephen Dorey ABIPP/Alamy; p.17 (illustration) Tim Bradley; pp.5 (bottom), 7 (top), 8–9 (background), 10 (top left), 11 (background), 16–17 (background), 18–19, 21 (bottom right), 22–23 (background), 24–25 (background), 26–27 (background), 30 iStock; p.12 (left) AFP/Getty Images/Newscom; pp.12–13 (background) NHPA/Photoshot/Newscom; pp.2–3, 31 Ton Koene/VWPics/Newscom; pp.6–7 Rob Blakers; p.25 (top) Jason Lin/Project TGIF; p.32 Ken Lax/Science Source; p.10 (bottom left) Martin Harvey/Science Source; p.10 (right) Nigel J. Dennis/Science Source; pp.28–29 (illustrations) J.J. Rudisill; all other images from Shutterstock.

Library of Congress Cataloging-in-Publication Data

Maloof, Torrey, author.
  People and the planet / Torrey Maloof.
    pages cm
  Summary: "We live on planet Earth. It gives us the things we need to survive. When it changes, it affects us all. But humans also affect Earth, and it's changing the planet we call home. It's important that we take care of our planet so it can continue to take care of us."--Provided by publisher.
  Audience: K to grade 3.
  Includes index.
  ISBN 978-1-4807-4650-3 (pbk.)
  ISBN 978-1-4807-5094-4 (ebook)
1. Human ecology—Juvenile literature.
2. Nature—Effect of human beings on—Juvenile literature.
3. Environmental protection—Juvenile literature. I. Title.
  GF48.M35 2015
  304.2'8—dc23
                                        2014034281

Teacher Created Materials
5301 Oceanus Drive
Huntington Beach, CA 92649-1030
http://www.tcmpub.com
ISBN 978-1-4807-4650-3

Table of Contents

Our Changing Planet

Imagine that each day you came home and found more people living in your house. What if they left trash lying around the house? What if they ate all the food in your kitchen? What if they started pulling boards out of the wall to build furniture? What if they burned the house down trying to stay warm? And what if billions of people around the world were all living this way?

The way we live does affect our home—Earth. Over time, our presence on Earth has changed it. Every day, we use its **natural resources**. We use the planet's water to grow our food. We use its oil to make fuel. We change the landscape of Earth's surface. We farm the land. We cut down forests to build homes. We change Earth's **atmosphere** with harmful substances released by cars and factories.

Scientists are learning that all these changes have serious consequences. People have lived on Earth for a long time. But we are just beginning to see the impact of our actions on our planet. We need to use its resources carefully. We need to make wise choices that will protect our planet.

Saving the Planet

Conservationists are people who work to protect land, plants, and animals. Conservationists find ways to conserve our natural resources.

The Earth is the only home we have.

We must work together to protect it.

Deforestation

One way people change the planet is by cutting down and removing trees from forests. This is called *deforestation*. There are many reasons trees are cut down. Trees are a natural resource. People cut down trees to use the wood to make paper and build homes. Wood can also be used to heat homes or cook food. The demand for wood and paper is high. So more forests are being cut down every day.

Some people clear forests to make room for crops. But after a few years, the soil may lose its **nutrients**. It's not as rich without trees. This makes it difficult for crops to grow there.

Before

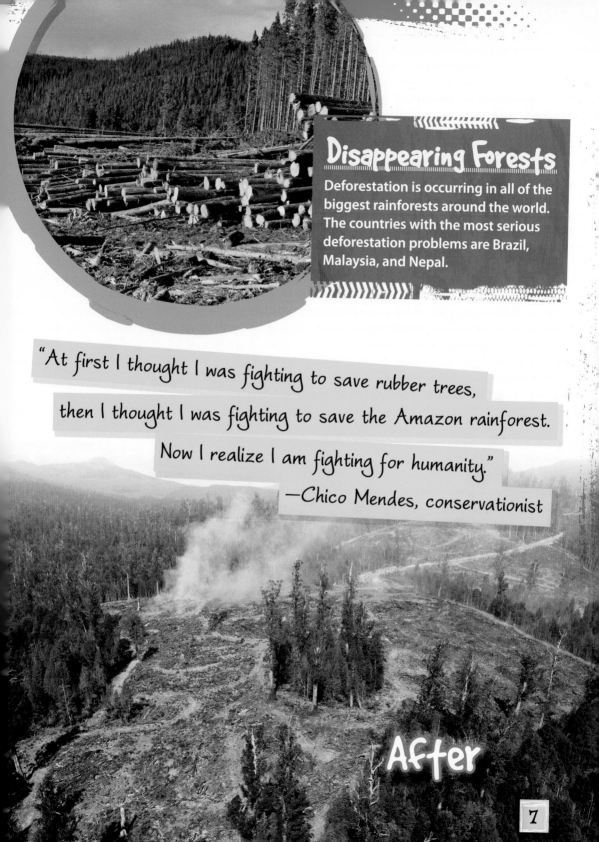

Disappearing Forests

Deforestation is occurring in all of the biggest rainforests around the world. The countries with the most serious deforestation problems are Brazil, Malaysia, and Nepal.

"At first I thought I was fighting to save rubber trees, then I thought I was fighting to save the Amazon rainforest. Now I realize I am fighting for humanity."
—Chico Mendes, conservationist

After

Deforestation is changing the entire planet. Seventy percent of land animals live in forests. When forests are cut down, these animals lose their homes. They may even become extinct, or die out. This can happen to plants, too.

Land **erosion** is also a problem. Tree roots hold soil in place. But when trees are cut down, soil loosens. This allows wind and water to wear away the land. The soil that is left will no longer absorb water. Instead, water rushes over it. This causes floods and landslides.

Trees also help us breathe. They do this by turning **carbon dioxide** into oxygen. We need oxygen to breathe. When forests are cut down, less oxygen is made. And there is more carbon dioxide in the air. This increases the **greenhouse effect**.

Planting new trees is one way to prevent deforestation.

The Consequences of Deforestation

Forests the size of Panama are being cut down every year. The consequences, such as floods and landslides, are dramatic.

increase in carbon dioxide

greenhouse effect

loss of nutrients in soil

difficulty growing crops

erosion

floods + landslides

loss of plant and animal homes

extinction

Desertification

The land on Earth is limited. We use this land for shelter and food. But sometimes, we overuse the land. We cut down too many trees. We pull too much water from the soil. When this happens, the land dries out. Soon, it can turn into a true desert. This process is called *desertification*.

Desertification

dry soil

lack of plants

overgrazing

Desertification is a natural process. It occurs by itself over time. But lately, humans have sped up the process. Today, it is happening all over the world. And it is happening quickly. The problem is more serious in areas with lots of people and a dry **climate**. These areas grow many crops. They also raise large numbers of animals. They do this to make sure there is enough food for everyone. But over time, this causes problems.

limited food

sand storms

Spreading South

There are two areas that are seriously suffering from desertification. One area is south of the Sahara Desert in Africa. The other area is south of the Gobi Desert in China.

Crops pull a lot of water and nutrients from soil. When an area does not get enough rain, soil becomes even drier. Soon, crops die. At the same time, farm animals graze on nearby plants. They can eat so many plants that the land grows bare. When crops die and there are no other plants left, soil loosens. This makes the land wear away quickly. The land becomes more desert-like.

More Trees, Please

Wangari Maathai (won-GAHR-ee muh-TAHY) hated seeing the effects of desertification near her home in Kenya. So, she worked with others to plant millions of trees. The trees helped prevent desertification. In 2004, she won a Nobel Peace Prize for her work.

One of the biggest problems of desertification is famine (FAM-in). Many people in these places do not have enough food to eat. And as more land turns to desert, there will not be enough good soil to grow crops.

Desertification also causes **droughts**. These long periods of dry weather make it even harder for plants and animals to survive. Some people must walk great distances to find drinking water. With little rain, the cycle continues and deserts grow larger.

A single cow can eat 18 kilograms (40 pounds) of food per day.

Pollution

It's not just the things we do directly to the land that change the planet. There are many things we do to make our lives easier and more fun that also damage the planet. We use electricity to light our homes at night. It helps us read when it is dark outside or play video games when it rains. Planes help us travel farther. They take us to faraway places for fabulous vacations. Cars help us go faster. They get us to school quickly or to a baseball game on time. We can take clean water with us everywhere we go thanks to plastic water bottles. These things help us and make life more enjoyable. But they also have a big impact on our planet.

Pollution is the process of making land, air, or water dirty and unsafe. Factories that make power often pollute the air. Cars and planes pollute the air, too. And plastic water bottles pollute the land.

Eliminating e-Waste

Digital or electronic devices such as TVs, batteries, or MP3 players can harm the environment when people dispose of them incorrectly. E-waste can leak dangerous chemicals into the ground and water. Cities often collect this waste on special days to help prevent pollution.

In one year, Americans use more than 50 billion plastic water bottles!

Every year, the number of people in the world rises. More people means more pollution. It means more trash ends up in our landfills. More toxic smoke enters the air. More **hazardous** waste mixes with our water. Pollution affects our planet in many ways, none of which are good. Today, pollution is a problem all around the world.

All living things need clean air to breathe and survive. Burning fossil fuels makes our air dirty. Factories burn fuel. We burn fuel when we use cars, trains, and planes. All of these things produce smoke, which pollutes the air with chemicals. The chemicals enter the atmosphere and mix with the rain. This polluted rain is called *acid rain*. Acid rain pollutes the ground and water. The water becomes harmful. This polluted water can damage plants and animals. It can also make humans sick.

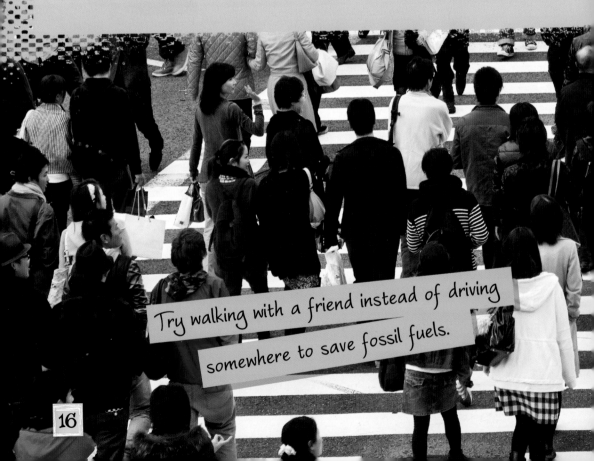

Try walking with a friend instead of driving somewhere to save fossil fuels.

Fossil Fuels

Coal, oil, and natural gas are fossil fuels. Fossil fuels are found in rocks deep in the ground. They take millions of years to make. They are made from the remains of dead plants and animals.

Fossil Fuel Formation

heat and pressure

heat and pressure

sediments

carbon from dead animals and plants

oil and gas deposits

The greenhouse effect is a natural process. But humans speed up the process by polluting the air. It is natural for carbon dioxide to be in the air. People and animals breathe it out. Carbon dioxide traps heat on Earth. Some of the heat escapes into space. Some heat returns to Earth. Just the right amount of heat helps keep our planet warm.

Natural Greenhouse Effect

Greenhouse Gases

solar radiation

reradiated heat

But when people burn fossil fuels, too much carbon dioxide is released into the air too quickly. When there is too much carbon dioxide in the air, too much heat gets trapped. This causes problems. Too much trapped heat can cause Earth's overall temperature to rise. This is known as *global warming*.

Harsh Changes

Scientists think global warming is responsible for these and other changes in the environment:
- higher temperatures
- intense weather
- more droughts
- shrinking sea ice

Human-Enhanced Greenhouse Effect

reradiated heat

solar radiation

reradiated heat

Terracing

People change the environment in many ways. But not all of them are bad. Terraces are large flat areas on hills or the sides of mountains. Building them is a simple, but powerful way to change the land.

In East and Southeast Asia, rice is an important part of nearly every meal. Rice is more nutritious than other grains, such as wheat. Rice has **carbohydrates**, which provide us with energy. However, growing rice is not easy. It requires a lot of hard work. But a small number of rice fields can feed a large number of people. Most of East and Southeast Asia consists of hills or mountains. This is not ideal farmland. To make it easier to grow crops, people have created terraces.

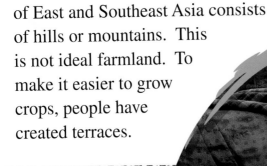

A farmer plants rice.

Thoughtful Farming

Terraces are used all across the world to grow many different things.

rice, wheat, and barley in Asia

corn in North America

potatoes in South America

olive trees in the Mediterranean

stalk of rice

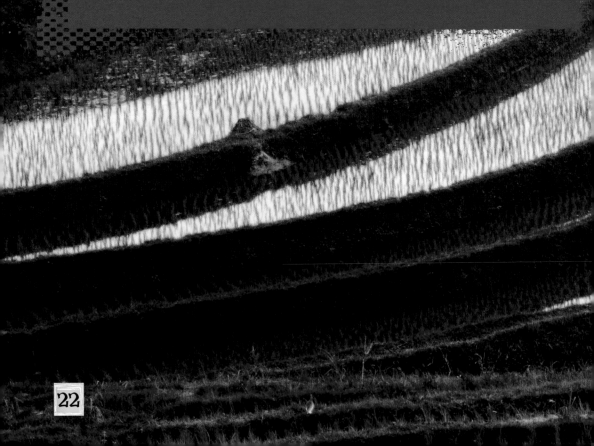

Terraces look like a series of steps carved into the land. They are mainly used for crops that need a lot of water, such as rice. Rice is grown in paddies, or flooded fields. Farmers must control the flow of water to grow rice. Terraces can help do this. If the paddies were on mountains without terraces, the water would just wash away. This would leave the rice shoots too dry to grow. Terracing changes the physical landscape of Earth. But it changes it in a good way. Terraces help hold rainwater. They keep the water from rushing downhill. This helps slow down erosion. It also helps to stop landslides and floods. Terraces also create farmland in areas that are not fit for farming. This helps to feed many people in areas where it is difficult to grow food.

Timeless Terraces

There are rice terraces in the Philippines that are more than 2,000 years old! They are the Banaue (BUH-now-ee) Rice Terraces. They cover more than 10,360 square kilometers (4,000 square miles) of land.

Rice comes in many colors and varieties.

Saving Our Planet

Our planet will stay the same size. It will not grow any larger. But every year, more and more people are living on Earth. The human family is growing in size. But our home is not. Experts wonder where everyone will live. Will there be enough food for everyone? What will we do with all of our trash? We depend on the planet for our survival. And the planet's survival depends on us.

Some people are finding new ways for us to live on Earth. They are called **environmentalists**. They have many ideas for how we can save our planet. They help farmers come up with new ways to grow crops and raise animals. They are finding ways to slow desertification. They teach people different ways to decrease pollution. They are also showing people why it is good to use natural forms of energy, such as wind or solar power.

COOKING OIL

Do Something

In 2008, fifth-grader Cassandra Lin started the project Turn Grease Into Fuel. She worked with other kids to collect cooking oil from local restaurants. They passed it on to families to use as inexpensive fuel for heating. The group has prevented more than two million pounds of carbon dioxide from entering the air.

You can help save our planet, too! You can reduce the amount of trash you make. Drink from glasses instead of plastic water bottles. Use boxes or fabric bags instead of plastic bags when you go shopping. And, you can recycle!

You can also turn off lights when they are not in use. This saves energy. You can ride your bike or walk to school. This helps reduce air pollution. You can also use less electricity by putting on a sweater instead of turning on a heater. These may seem like little things. But all these little things make a big difference.

We are still learning how to make the best use of the world we live in. What we have learned is that we need to take care of Earth because it takes care of us.

"It's the little things citizens do. That's what will make the difference. My little thing is planting trees."

—Wangari Maathai, conservationist

27

Think Like a Scientist

How do trees prevent soil erosion?
Experiment and find out!

What to Get

- damp sand
- small block
- tray
- twigs and grass
- water

What to Do

1 Pack damp sand into a shallow tray. Make sure the sand is level.

2 Prop one end of the tray up on a block.

3 Carve out a curvy line in the sand with your finger. Place twigs and grass along the line to represent trees.

4 Slowly pour water into the higher end of the line.

5 Record what happens as the water flows down the line. Note where erosion occurs and where it is avoided.

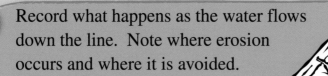

Glossary

atmosphere—the mass of air that surrounds Earth

carbohydrates—substances found in foods such as bread, rice, and potatoes which provide the human body with heat and energy

carbon dioxide—a gas that is produced when people and animals breathe out

climate—the usual type of weather a place gets

droughts—long periods of time with little or no rain

environmentalists—people who work to protect Earth from pollution and other threats

erosion—the process by which something wears away by natural forces such as water, wind, or ice

greenhouse effect—the natural warming of Earth's atmosphere

hazardous—dangerous or risky

natural resources—things existing in the natural world such as wood, oil, or minerals

nutrients—substances that living things need to live and grow

Index

Your Turn!

Help Our Planet

It's important that we take care of Earth because it takes care of us. Make a poster listing 10 things your community is doing to help save the environment. Share your findings with friends and family. Everyone can make a difference—including you!